JAZZ AGE POET

A Creative Minds Biography

JAZZ AGE POET

A Story about Langston Hughes

by Veda Boyd Jones

illustrations by Barbara Kiwak

M Millbrook Press/Minneapolis

To my Wednesday group—who have closed down a lot of restaurants

Text copyright © 2006 by Veda Boyd Jones
Illustrations copyright © 2006 by Barbara Kiwak

Millbrook Press
A division of Lerner Publishing Group
241 First Avenue North
Minneapolis, MN 55401   U.S.A.

Website address: www.lernerbooks.com

Library of Congress Cataloging-in-Publication Data

Jones, Veda Boyd.
    Jazz age poet : a story about Langston Hughes / by Veda Boyd Jones ; illustrations by Barbara Kiwak.—(A Creative Minds Biography)
        p.   cm.
    Includes bibliographical references and index.
    ISBN-13: 978–1–57505–757–6 (lib. bdg. : alk. paper)
    ISBN-10: 1–57505–757–3 (lib. bdg. : alk. paper)
    1. Hughes, Langston, 1902–1967—Juvenile literature. 2. Poets, American—20th century—Biography—Juvenile literature. 3. African American poets—Biography—Juvenile literature. I. Title.
    PS3515.U274Z665 2006
    818'.5209—dc22   2004028719

Manufactured in the United States of America
1 2 3 4 5 6 – JR – 11 10 09 08 07 06

Table of Contents

1

Passed-around Boy

Five-year-old Langston Hughes stared out the window of the southbound train and wondered what he would find at the end of the long ride. His mother and his grandmother were taking him to Mexico to meet his father.

He couldn't remember anything about his father. What would he look like? And what would it be like to live in a foreign country?

Langston's parents had separated shortly after he was born in Joplin, Missouri, on February 1, 1902. Sometimes he lived with his mother, Carrie, as she moved around looking for better jobs. Mostly, he lived with his grandmother, Mary Langston, in Lawrence, Kansas. He felt like a passed-around boy, but things were going to change. He could hardly wait to belong to a real family.

The train clickety-clacked its way into Mexico City. As it hissed to a slow stop, Langston pressed his face to the window and looked for his father.

The mustached stranger who met their train and kissed Carrie hello didn't smile much. When he talked, he barked orders. He said they'd stay at a hotel that night before traveling on to his home.

Langston had missed not having a father. He'd heard his mother and grandmother talking about James Hughes and how he had studied hard to be a lawyer. But because he was a black man, he was not allowed to take the test to become a lawyer. He had left the United States and headed to Mexico, where he said blacks were treated fairly. If a man worked hard there, he could make a good living, no matter what color his skin. And that's what he had done. Langston and his mother were there to see if they could find better lives too.

That night at the hotel, Langston awoke to find the bed shaking, but there was no one shaking it. A picture fell off the wall, and he screamed. His father yelled "earthquake," grabbed Langston, and carried him to the park across from the hotel. For nearly five minutes, the ground shook, and the noise of people screaming and buildings falling drowned out Langston's own cries. Terrified through the long night, Langston clung to his mother. At daylight he saw huge tarantulas crawling out of collapsed walls.

Carrie Hughes had seen enough. She wanted to go back to where people spoke English and there were no earthquakes. Langston and his mother and grandmother climbed on a train and went back to Kansas. His father remained in Mexico. Langston's dreams of a real home ended.

For a while, Langston stayed with his grandmother. But when his mother found a good job in Topeka, Kansas, she took her son with her to a new home. It was a one-room apartment above a plumbing shop.

Their small room held a one-burner cookstove. Langston gathered old crates in the alley behind stores. In the evenings, he and his mom chopped up the wooden boxes and used the pieces as fuel for the stove.

For their entertainment, Langston's mother read to him, and she spent some of her hard-earned money for movies and plays. Langston drank in the world of make-believe, where everyone was happy at the end of the story. He longed for this kind of storybook life and happy family.

Langston's real life was made harder by Jim Crow laws. These laws separated black people and white people in many parts of the country.

Blacks couldn't go into restaurants where white people ate. Blacks could only sit in the balcony at some movie theaters. At other theaters, they were not allowed inside at all. Blacks drank from certain public drinking fountains, while whites drank from different ones. Black children went to separate schools too.

When Langston was old enough for school, his mother took him to the nearby elementary school, but the principal said he could not attend the all-white school. He would have to go many blocks away to the black school. Carrie Hughes said this was not fair. She took her fight to the school board, and Langston was finally admitted to first grade at the white school.

At the white school, Langston sat at the end of the last row, even though the other students were seated in alphabetic order. His teacher didn't want him in the school, and she made hateful comments about his color. She stirred up the students with her remarks, such as warning them not to eat black licorice or they'd turn black like Langston. Some of them chased him home through alleys. He dodged the stones and tin cans they threw at him.

But one boy always defended Langston, and a few other classmates stood up for him. Their kindness taught Langston that people could be good regardless of the color of their skin.

Before school was out, Carrie took Langston back to live with his grandmother in Lawrence, and she moved to Colorado. Langston's grandmother lived near the University of Kansas in a tiny house in a mostly white section of town. She was fiercely proud. She refused to cook, clean, or wash for white people, the main jobs open to black women. Instead, she made money by renting out a room of her house to black students.

Langston's grandmother was over seventy and rarely left home. She made Langston stay home too. She didn't want him to play with the white boys in the neighborhood. He could hear the boys laugh and see them playing ball and marbles and tag. But he had to sit on the porch beside his grandmother rocking in her chair. She told him stories about people who spoke out to make sure black people had the same rights that white people did.

She told him about his grandfather, who had been an editor at an African American newspaper and started a literary society for blacks. She told him about his great-uncle, who was elected to Congress from Virginia.

Langston felt he was expected to be like his ancestors, to achieve something, to do something special with his life. But what special thing could he do?

He and his grandmother were very poor. Each month they struggled to find enough money to make the house payment and buy food. When things were really bad, they ate salt pork and wild dandelion greens. Langston lived in fear that they would lose the house and have nowhere to live and nothing to eat.

Every once in a while, Langston's mother would come for him. He visited her in Colorado. When she moved to Kansas City, Missouri, he sometimes rode the train to see her. He loved listening to the sounds of street life in the city, where black people sang the blues or laughed together on a street corner.

Life with his grandmother was lonely. Once he ran away from home. Another time he cried for his mother to come get him. He filled his spare time with reading and pretended he was the hero in stories. He wanted a life in which everything was perfect.

On long summer evenings when he wasn't reading, he'd sit on the front porch with his grandmother and listen to more tales of black history. In her stories, people triumphed or they failed, but they never cried. They worked, they planned, they tried new things. If they didn't succeed, they tried something else. They did not cry. So Langston learned to cry tears for his mother on the inside, but not on the outside for his grandmother to see.

Langston liked school because he wasn't so alone and could be around other children. But when he entered seventh grade in 1914, his teacher placed the few black students in a separate row. Langston, who was known for his easy laugh and pleasant ways, snapped. Fury mounted inside him. He was the grandnephew of a congressman, and his teacher was treating him like dirt. He couldn't stand it.

He printed "Jim Crow Row" on cards and placed them on each black student's desk. Then he ran onto the playground shouting that his teacher had a Jim Crow row. The principal grabbed him, and Langston punched him. He was expelled for his behavior. A group of black parents demanded he be allowed back in school. When Langston returned, the Jim Crow row was gone. His protest had been successful.

That same school year, when Langston was thirteen, his grandmother died. He moved in with her friends, whom he called Auntie and Uncle Reed. Auntie Reed tended her garden, cows, and chickens. Uncle Reed dug ditches and laid sewer pipe for the city. The Reeds owned their own home free and clear, which meant no one came around demanding money for a house payment. They ate good meals with garden vegetables and hoecakes of cornmeal with molasses and rich milk.

The Reeds were good to him. Auntie Reed was very religious and faithfully attended church. She insisted Langston attend with her. There he found a strange new world. He heard rousing spirituals and clapped his hands to the rhythms. He listened to the shouts from the amen corner, where worshippers called out loud when the spirit moved them. At the church, college students and community-minded folks read essays and poetry, listened to music, and discussed national events that affected African Americans. These discussion groups were his real introduction to "the Race," which is what he called black people.

Langston finally had a family of sorts, but he felt he was on the outside looking in. And he was still lonesome. He still dreamed of a time when his mother and father would come for him.

2

That Important Education

Life with Auntie and Uncle Reed was good. Langston was happier than when he had lived with his grandmother. He found a job and earned his first regular paycheck—fifty cents a week. He cleaned the toilets, the lobby, and the spittoons, the containers for spit, at a nearby hotel. It was dirty work, and he was quite sure his proud grandmother would have disapproved. But the pay allowed him to see movies.

One day the movie theater owner put up a sign, "NO COLORED ADMITTED." Langston was as angry as he was over the Jim Crow row at school, but this time he didn't speak out. He didn't know how to change the theater problem. He kept his anger inside and found new entertainment—road shows with singing and dancing and acting.

He adored the blues music he heard, with its melodies that cried and words that laughed. Sometimes the melodies tripped over themselves with happy rhythms and sad words. The blues were all mixed-up, and they echoed the song in his soul.

A few months later, Langston's mother sent for him. She had remarried. Her new husband's name was Homer Clark. Langston eagerly packed his few belongings for the trip to Lincoln, Illinois, and his new home and family. Homer already had a two-year-old son, and Langston thought of little Kit as a true brother.

At his new, mostly white school, Langston was voted class poet. He said it happened because most white people thought that all black people could sing and dance and had rhythm. Since a poem had to have rhythm—and he was black—his classmates saw a connection. Every one of them voted for him.

His duty as class poet was to write a poem for eighth-grade graduation. He struggled over the lines, writing something about each of the eight teachers and then about how wonderful his class was. When he read the poem at graduation, everyone applauded, and Langston enjoyed the approval.

To Langston's disappointment, however, his new stepfather was not in the audience to hear the poem.

Homer had left to find work. He was hired at a steel mill in Cleveland, Ohio, and he sent for the family. Langston moved once again.

In his new town, Langston began classes at Cleveland's Central High School. He found the mostly white school didn't pay attention to his color. Many of the students were from immigrant families from Europe and Asia, and they were minorities too. Finally, Langston fit in. His ready smile and easy ways made him many friends. He was elected to the student council, and he ran on the track team. He also wrote more poems. Some were published in the school's magazine.

Langston was feeling secure, but the happy family he yearned for was only a dream. During Langston's second year in high school, Homer and Carrie separated. Carrie moved to Chicago, leaving Langston living alone in a rooming house to finish the school year. As soon as the school year was over, he joined Carrie and Kit in Chicago. On his first Sunday there, he explored the city and wandered into a whites-only area. A group of white boys told him they didn't allow his kind in their neighborhood and attacked him. Langston endured the beating and was so ashamed of it, that he didn't tell his mother. He desperately wanted to go back to Cleveland, where he fit in.

The hot summer in the city dragged on and on. During the day, Langston worked as a delivery boy for a hat shop. He saved money for his return to school in Cleveland. At night he lay in the hot bedroom and was jarred awake again and again as trains rumbled past.

When summer was finally over, Langston prepared to go back to school in Cleveland. His mother didn't want him to go. She wanted Langston to quit school so he could work and earn money to support her and Kit. But Langston argued with his mother. He pointed out to her that without education he couldn't get a job that would pay very much.

Carrie gave in, and Langston returned to Cleveland. With little money, he rented an attic room, and he lived on rice and hot dogs. They were cheap and easy to cook. He studied hard and learned to read French, which he thought made him seem very smart. He wrote more poems. He was lonesome, so very lonesome, and he poured his heart into his words.

At the end of Langston's third year in high school, his father wrote and demanded that he come to Mexico for the summer. Langston, filled with hope, took the long train ride south. But once again his dream of a united family disappeared.

His father's favorite phrase was "hurry up!" His

father hurried to make money. He hated poor people because they hadn't hurried to make money as he did. He thought most black people were lazy because they didn't hurry like he did. He hated them too.

It seemed that everything Langston loved in the world, his father hated. James Hughes hated poems. He had no use for them. He wanted Langston to study accounting, but Langston didn't like math.

His father's way of hating rubbed off, and Langston decided he hated his father. Feeling it was useless to show his anger, Langston kept it bottled up inside him until he was physically ill and ended up in a hospital.

When he was well enough to travel, he rode the train back to Cleveland. Blacks had to sleep sitting up on the train. Langston, who was fairly light-skinned, said he was Mexican. That way he was able to get a sleeping berth as the train rattled through Texas. Once Langston reached Saint Louis, a soda fountain clerk at the train station asked him if he were Mexican or black. Langston admitted he was black, and the clerk turned his back on him. Langston was sad to see that his father was right about how blacks were treated in the United States.

On that train ride to Cleveland, Langston thought about his parents. His father wanted Langston around just so he could tell him how he should live.

His mother wanted him around so he could help her out with money. Her idea was to spend money for enjoyment. His father's idea was to make money to save it. There had to be something in between.

And what about their attitudes toward the Race? His father hated blacks, and his mother seemed bitter about being black. Where did that leave Langston? Maybe it was time Langston admitted that his parents would never be there for him and quit dreaming about a happy family that never would be.

During his last year in high school, Langston set out to be his own person. He joined groups and wrote poetry. When writing, Langston felt fulfilled. In his writing, he could shout for black people with the tones he had heard at Auntie Reed's church. He had learned about important black people from his grandmother. He had found his writer's voice. It reflected the stories of the black people in his life.

After he graduated, Langston yearned to go to college. But where in the world could he get the money? The only wealthy person he knew was his father. He pushed the previous awful summer to the back of his mind and went against his mother's pleas. He climbed on the train heading south.

The train reached Saint Louis and began the long crossing of the Mississippi River. Langston stared at the muddy waters. Words came to him from deep inside. He jotted a poem on the back of an envelope. He wrote about knowing old rivers. He tried to write it as if he were the entire black race growing up beside rivers in different parts of the world.

At his father's Mexican home, Langston asked if he could go to Columbia University in New York City. James Hughes thought college was a good idea if Langston went to Europe where blacks were not treated so badly and if he studied to be an engineer.

But Langston wanted to be a writer. Writing made him happy. He decided he would have to put himself through college so he could be what he wanted to be. To earn money, he taught English at a private school in Mexico. In his spare time, he wrote. He sent two poems to *Brownie's Book,* an African American children's magazine. They were accepted for publication. He showed the magazine to his father.

His father saw his son's name in print on the poems. He asked Langston how much he was paid. Nothing, Langston admitted, but it wouldn't always be that way. He wanted to make a living as a writer.

He sent his poem about rivers to the *Crisis,* an adult magazine for African Americans, and it was published. After seeing that poem in print, his father agreed to send Langston to Columbia University.

Langston stood on the deck of the ship that had taken him away from Mexico. He grinned ear to ear when he caught his first glimpse of New York City. He took the subway to the area known as Harlem and saw black people everywhere. He had found a home.

Columbia University was a different story. When he arrived at the dorm, he was denied a room because of his color. His application had been postmarked from Mexico, so school officials thought he was Mexican. Never before had a black person lived in the dorms. But Langston produced his dorm assignment letter and was allowed to unpack.

Langston didn't fit in at Columbia. The courses weren't too hard. It was just that he would rather be in Harlem watching plays, hearing the blues sung on street corners, and laughing and talking with the black people around him. At the Harlem library, he met another young poet, Countee Cullen. At the *Crisis* office, he met the editor, W. E. B. Du Bois.

Jazz and ragtime poured from the clubs. Harlem was growing, celebrating, experiencing a boom in literature, music, and theater. Langston was in the midst of the Harlem Renaissance, as it came to be called.

He drew energy from the people around him in Harlem, not from the other students at Columbia. At the end of his first year of college, Langston dropped out.

He looked for work and finally found a job on a farm on Staten Island. The outdoor work suited him fine. He planted, hoed, watered, and harvested beets, carrots, onions, and lettuce until Labor Day. Briefly, he took a job delivering flowers. Then he decided to see the world.

He took a job as a ship's mess boy, helping the cook. Langston had great hopes of going abroad. Instead, the ship headed up the Hudson River and anchored at Jones Point, New York, for the winter. His ship tended the unused warships that were anchored there.

Langston oiled machinery and checked cables on the abandoned ships. The isolation was perfect for his writing. He passed the cold winter reading books and writing more poems.

By spring he was ready for a change. He applied to other ships and in June boarded a ship bound across the wide Atlantic Ocean for Africa.

The ship set sail, and Langston and other sailors unpacked their bags. As he was taking his books out of a box, an unexpected urge grabbed hold of Langston. He carried his books to the deck. One by one, he threw them overboard. As each one sank in the deep ocean, he felt lighter and lighter. He was throwing away memories of escaping into books as a child and of studying at college. No longer would he escape from his own life through books. He would live it.

He saved only one book, a book of poetry. It symbolized what he wanted to do with his life.

3

Traveling Man

As Langston's ship carried him across the Atlantic Ocean to Africa, his excitement mounted. At last, he would see the homeland of the black race that he so admired. Except for his time in Harlem and Chicago, he'd lived in mostly white neighborhoods, and there he had been an outcast. Finally, he hoped, he'd be accepted in Africa.

His first glimpse of Africa stirred excitement in

him. Here was the motherland of the black race, where he was sure he belonged. His heart pounded as he stepped on land and talked with black African people. But the Africans would not believe he was one of them.

Langston had light brown skin. He was a mix of white, Indian, and black ancestors. Many black Africans said he was a white man. Langston was lost. His hopes of being accepted were dashed. In America he didn't fit into the white world because his skin was brown. In Africa he didn't fit into the black world for the same reason.

He met a young boy with a similar problem. The son of a black African woman and a white Englishman, the boy was shunned by both blacks and whites. The boy asked if it were true that black people in America were friendly to people of mixed races. And was it true that white people treated them badly?

Langston told him that most American blacks were friendly to people like him. But he didn't have an easy answer about how whites treated people of mixed race. Whites had been kind to him, and whites had beaten him up. He decided friendliness depended on the kind of person someone was inside, instead of the color of the skin.

When his ship returned to the United States, Langston visited his mother. Then he returned to Harlem, where he wrote poems and worried about his future. He wanted to go to college, but not back to Columbia. He wanted a black college where he would be accepted. Since the college term had already started and he had no money for tuition, Langston signed on as mess boy with another ship.

The Atlantic Ocean crossing was rough, with cold, miserable weather. The return trip to New York was the same, but Langston signed on for another trip. This voyage to Europe was even worse. A sailor died of pneumonia and was buried at sea. A mess boy's foot was badly scalded. And the wireless radio operator went crazy, refusing to leave his room. Langston took these as signs that the ship might be jinxed.

After the ship docked in Holland, he collected his pay and left. He took a train to France and worked as a dishwasher at a Paris nightclub. He kept writing poetry and sending it to magazines in New York. Sometimes he didn't know where his next meal was coming from, but he always managed.

Langston went on vacation to Italy with two waiters from the restaurant, who were going to visit their families. He was greeted enthusiastically as the first black person ever to visit the town.

Soon after, he decided it was time to go back to the United States. On the train trip to a port city, a pickpocket stole his wallet and his passport. Langston was stranded in Genoa, Italy, for nearly a month. He hung out at the wharf, waiting for a ship sailing for home that would hire him. But ship after ship turned him away because he was black. During this time, he wrote the poem, "I, Too, Sing America," which foretells a time when blacks and whites would be equal.

A ship with an all-black crew finally took him on as a working passenger. He had to chip old paint off the vessel to pay for his voyage, but at last, he was on his way home.

Back in Harlem that first night, he looked up Countee Cullen. They went to a benefit party for the National Association for the Advancement of Colored People (NAACP). To Langston's surprise, he found that the people there knew his poetry. In the ten months he'd been in Europe, the *Crisis* and other magazines had been publishing his poems. That night he also saw Du Bois again. He met James Weldon Johnson, secretary of the NAACP and an accomplished writer of fiction and poetry. He also met Arna Bontemps, a young black writer who would become Langston's lifelong friend, and one white writer, popular novelist Carl Van Vechten.

Langston's mother and stepbrother were now living with wealthy cousins in Washington, D.C. Langston left New York and stayed with them for a while. He quickly found that he didn't like people of the black upper class like his relatives. He found them consumed by thoughts about their money and position, just like his father.

He moved his mother and brother into two unheated rooms in Washington and worked at a few odd jobs. He wrote more poetry than ever before. He discovered that when he was unhappy, he produced poetry. When he was happy, he rarely wrote.

During this difficult time, more and more of his poetry was published in magazines. He wrote about his feelings of having black and white ancestors.

In Langston's day, he was called a mulatto. He explored the multiracial theme that kept going through his mind.

Langston also listened to the music being played on the streets in the poor neighborhoods. One day he was singing as he walked along, and a man asked him if he were hurt. Langston told him he was just singing, and the man said he was sorry, he thought he was groaning. Langston never sang on the street again, but he continued to try to catch the rhythm of the songs in his poetry.

Opportunity magazine held a literary contest. Langston entered several pieces in the contest. One was "The Weary Blues," a poem he had started years earlier when he was on the boat anchored on the Hudson River. He had reworked and reworked it to get the rhythm of the blues, with the music's haunting sadness.

Langston rode the train to New York for the dinner at which the winner would be announced. Every big publishing house in New York had a representative there. Also present were Countee Cullen, Zora Neale Hurston—a young black woman who wrote short stories—and Carl Van Vechten, the white writer Langston had met on his first night back from Europe.

When the moment arrived for the announcement of the poetry winners, Langston caught his breath. He could hardly believe it when his name was called. "The Weary Blues" had won first prize.

Carl Van Vechten crossed the room and congratulated Langston. He invited him to his apartment the next day and asked if Langston could bring other poems. Several black poets shied away from the white man, but Langston had been around whites most of his life. He had a notebook full of poems to share.

The next day, he read a few of his poems aloud and

left a few others for Van Vechten to read. Van Vechten liked Langston's work and was amazed at the way he captured the blues in poetry form. He said he'd try to find a publisher for a book of Langston's poetry.

Langston chose the poems that would work best in a book and submitted them to Van Vechten. Van Vechten took the collection to his publisher. Langston received a contract from the respected publisher Alfred A. Knopf just eighteen days after the *Opportunity* contest dinner.

Langston couldn't believe his good fortune. He was about to have a book published, and he was only twenty-three years old.

4

Finding His Way

Reading the proofs, the first printed version of his book, Langston worried whether black people would like it. He wondered if black readers would reject the book because Van Vechten, a white man, wrote the introduction. Maybe not, he decided. After all, his poems were not just for black people.

Desperate for money, he took a job as a busboy at a Washington hotel. Well-known poet Vachel Lindsay stayed at the hotel when he was in the area for poetry readings. Langston decided to meet the man. He copied three of his poems in his neatest handwriting. When Lindsay came in the dining room for dinner, Langston walked to his table and laid down the poems. He mumbled something about admiring the poet's work.

That night during his reading, Lindsay announced that he had discovered a black poet. He read all three of Langston's poems. The next morning, reporters asked Langston about his poetry, and the story made national newspapers. Langston hoped the publicity would help his book sell lots of copies.

He was writing more poems than ever before, but he had not given up his dream of going to college. When he won prizes in another poetry contest, he wrote a thank-you note to the sponsor. She was a wealthy white woman named Amy Spingarn, who gave money to the NAACP. He told her he hoped to go to college, but he didn't have the money. She replied that he should visit her in Manhattan, and they would talk about it. At their meeting, the two spoke of his hopes and dreams. He said he wanted to go to a black college. The day before Christmas 1925, Langston opened a letter from her. It awarded him a scholarship to Lincoln College in Pennsylvania. He said it was the best Christmas present he'd ever had.

While waiting for the new semester to begin, Langston quit his job at the Washington hotel and worked on his poems. His mother would not let him eat at home because he wasn't working to help her out with money. She was angry that he would be away at college and not working for several more years.

Langston loved Lincoln College. There were three hundred black men enrolled. He quickly joined a social club, took part in lighthearted pranks, swapped clothes with friends, and cheered at football games. He wrote Carl Van Vechten that Lincoln was more like home should be than any place he'd ever been. The spirit of friendship and cooperation made him happy.

He had a room to himself because school officials knew he needed to be alone to write. But Langston didn't only write poetry. He wrote an essay for the *Nation* magazine about the black artist. He felt that many black writers were trying to write like white people and that meant not claiming their own race. He wrote that poets should not be afraid to be themselves. For Langston Hughes, writing about black people was a part of being himself.

Soon Langston had a second book of poetry published, and he began reading his poems to groups, usually at black churches. At times four college students would sing in the background. Langston thought the harmony helped accent the blues rhythms in his poems.

Some weekends, Langston took the train to New York City. He went to the theater and to blues clubs. He visited with his writer friends and attended parties.

At one party, he met a well-dressed older white woman who was interested in African American artists. Charlotte Mason liked Langston and invited him to visit her in her Manhattan apartment. Through the spring, they talked whenever he was in New York. By November 1927, Mrs. Mason became his patron. She gave him $150 a month to live on and to encourage his art. All he had to do was account for his money and write.

Mason also demanded that Langston call her Godmother, which was fine with him. He thought of her as a fairy godmother. She made it possible for him to have nice clothes, fine seats at plays, and chauffeur-driven rides back to college after visits to her in the city.

He loved her as he never had loved his own grandmother. He felt as if he were part of a family. The two dined on rich foods and talked for hours about the black world and art. She told him what he should be writing. She wanted a novel, so Langston started one.

Godmother continued her patronage even after Langston graduated from college in 1929. He completed his novel and settled in a little house in Westfield, New Jersey. Then he took off for Cuba for a restful vacation.

In Cuba he was hailed as the great American black poet. Langston explained to the Cubans that he lived among the blacks in the United States, and he wrote about their troubles and their sorrows. He knew of these things because he was one of them.

With money from Godmother, Langston was not hurt by the Depression that arrived in 1929. The economy was bad then and many people were out of work.

But not long after his return from Cuba, he fell out of favor with his patron. He heard through a friend that she thought he was not writing enough. He was working on a play.

He had explained to her he wanted to make his own decisions on what to write. But he also wanted her affection and support. He wrote a long apology letter. This smoothed things over for a while. He made sure to send her the first copy of his novel, *Not without Laughter.* But then the final break came. Langston was stunned.

He could not remember much of that last time in her apartment above Park Avenue because it reminded him too much of the time in Mexico when he decided he hated his father. Charlotte Mason felt he was wasting his time and her money by not writing more.

Langston knew that he had to work in his own way and at his own speed. But he swallowed words he wanted to speak. He held them inside where they rolled around in his stomach and caused great pain.

The loneliness of his childhood, when no one was there for him, crept back into his mind. He felt alone again, so he returned to his mother's home in Cleveland, Ohio.

On top of Charlotte Mason's rejection, his publisher had rejected his latest poems. He finished a play, *Mulatto,* but he didn't feel it was his best work. Then he was awarded four hundred dollars and a medal for distinguished achievement among blacks in literature. Winning this made him believe in himself again. It was the most money he had ever had at one time, and it made him think he could make a living as a writer. He used the money to return to Cuba with Zell Ingram, an artist friend. Then he went on to the mostly black country of Haiti to gain experiences to write about and to think about his future without Godmother's help.

Langston and Zell returned to the United States by way of Florida. There they met with the president of a black woman's college, Mary McLeod Bethune. She treated them to dinner and told them she was planning to go north, so she'd just ride along with them.

On the road, the trio shared a single bench seat in a small car. They laughed and talked and never grumbled about how cramped it was or how hot it was. Mary Bethune knew people all along their route, so when it came time to eat, they stopped at her friends' homes. Sometimes she arranged for Langston to read his poetry.

By the end of the trip, Mary Bethune had convinced Langston that he should travel throughout the South reading his poems. He wondered if he could make a living that way. He remembered that poet Vachel Lindsay had been on tour reading his poems when they had met at the hotel. But would southern blacks pay hard-earned money to hear him when jobs were so hard to get? It was worth a chance, he decided.

5

Moving Around

Langston's plan of bringing poetry to the South needed start-up money. He applied for and received a grant from a foundation that aided black education. It gave him a thousand dollars for the tour. He bought a car with the money, even though he couldn't drive. Then he convinced a friend to be his driver for part of the profits of the tour. He wrote letters to colleges, organizations, churches—anywhere that people might be willing to pay to hear a black poet read his poems. As expected, many places turned him down, but others hired him.

Besides the reading fee, he had books to sell. The fees he earned kept him moving along. Black people loved hearing one of their own reading his poetry.

The tour showed Langston the separate lives led by African Americans in the South. Jim Crow laws were still strongly enforced there. Blacks and whites were made to live separately. Many times Langston had to enter the place he was speaking at through the back door. Many restaurants refused to serve him, and he couldn't stay at whites-only hotels.

When the tour ended, Langston had a chance to travel to Russia. He was asked to work on a film about African Americans that was going to be shot there. The film was never made, but Langston stayed on and found more work in Russia as a writer. He wrote essays for a Russian newspaper and sent short stories back to New York magazines.

He had seen blacks treated badly in the United States, in Africa, and in Europe. But in Russia, they were treated with respect.

Russia was part of the Soviet Union, a Communist country. The government controlled all businesses and owned all property. Everyone received the same pay. According to Communists' ideas, people—black or white—worked for the good of everyone, and all were equal.

When his travel permit expired, Langston returned home by way of Japan, China, and Hawaii. He arrived in California nearly a year after his around-the-world journey had begun. He admired the equality he saw in the Soviet Union. He wrote poems that made many people think he accepted Communist ideas. He wanted equality for black people. He wondered if Communism was a way to achieve it.

A wealthy white man, Noel Sullivan, who shared Langston's beliefs, became his new patron. Sullivan owned a cabin in Carmel, California. He offered it to Langston for a year, with a cook and groceries provided. Langston set a goal of writing one short story a week. He wrote steadily mornings and early afternoons. Then he'd take a long walk on the beach and return to meet with the local people at parties.

But Langston was lonely. He was living among white people once again, distancing himself from his own people. Even with new friends, he felt alone.

As his year at the cabin drew to a close, he decided to move to Reno, Nevada. He lived briefly in a rented room. There he wrote stories about whites and published them under a pen name so that no one would know a black man had written them. He had often criticized black poets for not writing about their own people, but he needed money.

When news came that his father had died, Langston borrowed money from his father's sister for a trip to Mexico. He wanted to be there for the reading of his father's will. His aunt hoped there might be an inheritance for both of them. But his father had left his property and his money to some friends in Mexico. These friends insisted that Langston was entitled to one-fourth of the inheritance.

With that money, Langston lived for six months in Mexico, meeting Mexican writers. He translated their works into English and tried to get them published in the United States. After that, Langston returned to California, traveled about a bit, and landed in Ohio, where his mother was still living.

When he learned that his play, *Mulatto,* was being produced on Broadway, he headed to New York to oversee it. The play had been changed from the way he'd written it. He argued with the producer, the person putting on the play, about changing it back, but he got nowhere. The producer even told Langston he would have to pay for his ticket to the play's opening night. The producer arranged for all blacks to be seated in a separate section and excluded all black people, including Langston and black actors, from the opening night party. Langston was so angry that he didn't attend the opening.

In that state of mind, he learned that his mother had cancer. He moved back to Ohio to be with her. While in Ohio, he wrote plays and had them produced, but he made very little money. His mother thought he was rich, since he was a well-known writer. He told her he actually wasn't making a lot of money. She asked him why he didn't get a regular job.

Just as he'd told his father years ago, he explained that he wanted to make his living as a writer. He had already learned that most writers worked other jobs to support themselves, but that wasn't for him. He wanted to live a life that allowed his creativity to soar. But, as a compromise, he took a job that involved writing.

Langston signed up as a newspaper correspondant to cover the Civil War in Spain. The Spanish people were fighting to be free, and Langston wanted to be near the action. Many Americans stepped up to fight in Spain.

In June 1937, he sailed for Europe. He walked the familiar streets of Paris and gave a speech at the International Writers' Congress being held there. He spoke on racial issues and wondered aloud why blacks, who did not have equal rights at home, would risk their lives to help ensure freedom for Spaniards.

In Spain, Langston discovered that blacks fought

alongside whites. They were equals in this war. With sniper bullets zinging around him, with bombs going off near the hotel where he was staying, with death all around him, Langston was scared. Yet he felt strangely free. Along with his newspaper articles, he was inspired to write poetry about the triumph of the human spirit.

Six months later, he returned home to find his mother's health failing. He had to earn some money to support her. Again, he relied on a reading and lecture tour for quick cash. He found a group willing to produce some of his plays, rented an apartment in Harlem, and moved his mother in with him. When his mother died, Langston borrowed money for her funeral. He was thirty-six years old, and he was an orphan.

During his youth, he was passed around—from his mother to his grandmother to Auntie and Uncle Reed to his father and to his mother again. As an adult, he had also moved from place to place, searching for something. Perhaps it was a sense of belonging or a permanent home. It was time to find out who he really was.

6

The Writing Life

To find out who he was, Langston had to under-stand his past. What better way, he thought, than to write his autobiography. Carl Van Vechten and Arna Bontemps had suggested the idea to him. He started the project with enthusiasm. In *The Big Sea,* he wrote about how his father's demands had made him physi-cally sick, how his mother wanted him to quit his edu-cation to earn a living for her, and how hurt he was by Godmother's rejection.

In the book, he acknowledged that he could not have made his living by writing if not for various peo-ple who helped through the years. He looked back on his life and realized that, without patrons, he was always broke. He saw that he had lived his life with-out a real sense of family, and he wanted both a fam-ily and a comfortable living.

He sought out a longtime friend of his mother, "Aunt" Toy Harper. She and her husband, Emerson, had stored Langston's belongings for him when he left New York. He reached out to them as the parents he had always wanted. He called their small apartment his home base.

He tried to make a comfortable living by juggling projects—plays, poetry, and prose. He had written essays for the *Chicago Defender,* an African American weekly. He was asked to write a column. It was not a lot of money, but it was steady. He continued to rely on speaking tours for income.

At first, he wrote about many different things in his column. Then one evening, he met a man at a bar who had a lot to say on the subject of human nature, on being black, and on coping in a prejudiced world. From this chance meeting, Langston created the character Jesse B. Semple, called Simple. Langston made up conversations with Simple, and in his columns he let the man speak in his own words and give his own opinions.

Langston claimed he was just talking to himself. Simple's tone was Langston's tone. Simple wasn't a fighter, but he confronted the everyday problems that African Americans faced with humor and sometimes a quiet desperation.

Many educated blacks disliked Langston's Simple stories. They claimed the stories presented African Americans in a bad light. But Langston defended his work. He said it showed the world how the majority of black people lived and what they thought.

He had another chance to voice black issues when he took part in a live segment of *America's Town Meeting of the Air,* an NBC radio debate show. Langston represented the black view in a program on race relations. The speakers debated whether the government should step in and end Jim Crow laws. Although his voice shook with nervousness at first, he soon felt at ease in front of the studio audience.

Langston did a good job thinking on his feet and representing the black community. He was offered other speaking jobs in front of white audiences as well as black. By speaking all across the nation, he became the best-known black poet in the land.

He taught one semester as a visiting professor of writing at Atlanta University, a black college. His stay in Atlanta was wonderful, except for the Jim Crow laws.

He was once stranded at the airport for several hours because no taxi would pick up an African American man. He was hungry because the lunch counter wouldn't serve an African American.

Langston Hughes was famous, but he was still just getting by financially. Then, with Uncle Emerson and Aunt Toy Harper, he purchased a three-story brownstone in Harlem. Aunt Toy and Uncle Emerson lived in part of it and rented out extra rooms. Langston set up an office and home on the top floor.

He had to trudge up two flights of stairs, but it was a place to call home. He fell into a happy routine. He woke at noon, showered, and ate one of Aunt Toy's breakfasts. Then a part-time secretary helped him answer letters. He met with visitors or attended outside appointments. In the evenings, he went to plays, readings, parties, bars, always somewhere, returning to the third floor around two in the morning. Then he began writing. With no interruptions, he'd write until dawn. After the sun rose, he'd step out for the morning newspaper. Then he'd go to sleep, awaken about noon, and start the new day.

At last, he felt in control of his own life. He kept good records of his writing expenses and income and his speaking engagements. He liked his new life, but soon his past crept up on him.

In the 1950s, some people in the United States were afraid that Communists might try to take over the country. The Communists in the Soviet Union had taken away people's rights and freedom. The U.S.

Senate formed a committee to investigate Communist activity in the United States. Many people were called to testify. Because he had written poems in praise of the Soviet Union when he lived there in his twenties, Langston was called before the committee. He testified that he had never joined the Communist Party. He said that his poetry only reflected his thoughts and his ideas.

Although he was not charged with a crime, Langston's reputation was hurt. Lectures were canceled, and book sales slowed. Still, Langston kept working. He wrote several nonfiction books for children. One introduced black role models, such as poet Paul Laurence Dunbar, scientist George Washington Carver, and Nobel Peace Prize winner Ralph Bunche. He also worked on another autobiography about his travels around the world.

Langston was on vacation in Puerto Rico when he received a telegram informing him that he would receive the Spingarn Award. This medal was given yearly at the NAACP convention and honored high and noble achievement by an African American.

At the ceremony, he accepted the award in the name of all black people. He said that their hopes and fears and dreams were in his stories, poems, plays, and songs.

Langston edited a book of poems by new African American writers, including works by Mari Evans, Calvin Hernton, and Jay Wright. He encouraged young writers such as Alice Walker, Paule Marshall, and Loften Mitchell. He felt it was time for younger people to take their place in literature.

A violent struggle for black civil rights began in the 1960s. Langston avoided the demonstrations and sit-ins by black groups protesting Jim Crow laws. Most of his life, he had stayed away from fights, and he could not join in now. He stopped writing his Simple columns, but reprinted them in several books. He felt Simple no longer represented the African American voice because times were angrier.

Even without the column, Langston was constantly busy. He went on speaking tours to European and African countries for the U.S. State Department. When he returned after four months away from the United States, he jumped into a variety of projects— some editing, some poetry, and another nonfiction book for children.

In May 1967, Langston felt a pain in his lower stomach. He was admitted to the hospital and later underwent surgery. An infection set in after the surgery, and it quickly traveled through his body. He died from the massive infection on May 22, 1967.

Earlier, he had told friends that he wanted jazz and blues played at his funeral. They honored his wishes.

People at his funeral didn't know whether to laugh or cry. They did a bit of both as mournful blues and toe-tapping jazz were played by a group of his friends. The memorial service was a celebration of Langston's life. His friends decided he wanted them to laugh and cry at the same time, the way the blues had made him feel.

Through his many writings—poems, stories, plays, essays, articles, novel, and nonfiction books—Langston left his readers with this message: every life is to be lived with its struggles and pain, but not without laughter.

Selected Bibliography

Haskins, James S. *Always Movin' On: The Life of Langston Hughes.* New York: Franklin Watts, 1976.

Hughes, Langston. *The Big Sea.* New York: Hill and Wang, 1963. First published 1940 by Alfred A. Knopf.

Hughes, Langston. *I Wonder as I Wander: An Autobiographical Journey.* New York: Rinehart, 1956.

Hughes, Langston. *Selected Poems of Langston Hughes.* New York: Alfred A. Knopf, 1959.

Meltzer, Milton. *Langston Hughes: A Biography.* New York: Thomas Y. Crowell Company, 1968. Reprinted as *Langston Hughes: An Illustrated Edition.* Brookfield, CT: Millbrook Press, 1997.

Osofsky, Audrey. *Free to Dream: The Making of a Poet: Langston Hughes.* New York: Lothrop, Lee & Shepard Books, 1996.

Rampersad, Arnold. *The Life of Langston Hughes.* 2 vols. 2nd ed. New York: Oxford University Press, 2002.

Rhynes, Martha E. *I, Too, Sing America: The Story of Langston Hughes.* Greensboro, NC: Morgan Reynolds, 2002.

Index

About the Author

Veda Boyd Jones enjoys the challenge of writing both fiction and nonfiction for readers of different ages. She is the author of thirty-seven books, most of them for young people. She received history degrees from Crowder College, Pittsburg State University, and the University of Arkansas. Veda and her husband, Jimmie, the best architect in Joplin, Missouri, have three sons. For fun, Veda enjoys sailing on Grand Lake in Oklahoma and playing board games with friends.

About the Illustrator

Barbara Kiwak, graduating from the Maryland Institute College of Art in 1988 with a BFA in Visual Communications, began her career as an illustrator. Some of her clients include Time Life, *Reader's Digest*, *Highlights for Children*, The World Wildlife Fund, and Parker Brother's. Recently, Kiwak has been pursuing a more fine art career. She has had numerous showings in the Baltimore/Washington area, including The Life of Maryland Gallery, the Howard County Center For the Arts, and the Gudelsky Gallery in Washington DC.

For more information about Kiwak and her work, log onto www.Kiwak.com